SONS OF PROPHETS

FIELD GUIDES FOR THE SUPERNATURAL

Practical Steps for Navigating
the Spiritual Realm

Spiritual Field Guides: Practical steps for navigating the spiritual realm

Paperback ISBN: 978-1-966354-40-6

Sons of Prophets Publishing

PO Box 575 | Pickerington, OH 43147

sonsofprophets.com

| 10 9 8 7 6 5 4 3 2 1 |

Published in the United States of America

FIELD GUIDES FOR THE SUPERNATURAL

Table of Contents

KEYS TO HEARING GOD

CULTIVATING A LIFESTYLE OF DIVINE COMMUNICATION

God is not silent, He speaks to His people. This guide is designed to help you discern, recognize, and respond to His voice with clarity and confidence.

For free guides and resources, scan this qr code to download the Sons of Prophets app.

Biblical Foundation

God Still Speaks

Hebrews 1:1–2 NASB

God, after He spoke long ago to the fathers in the prophets in many portions and in many ways, in these last days has spoken to us in His Son, whom He appointed heir of all things, through whom He also made the world.

Acts 10:10-16 NASB

But he became hungry and was desiring to eat; but while they were making preparations, he fell into a trance; and he *saw the sky opened up, and an object like a great sheet coming down, lowered by four corners to the ground, and there were in it all kinds of four-footed animals and crawling creatures of the earth and birds of the air. A voice came to him, "Get up, Peter, kill and eat!" But Peter said, "By no means, Lord, for I have never eaten anything unholy and unclean." Again a voice came to him a second time, "What God has cleansed, no longer consider unholy." This happened three times, and immediately the object was taken up into the sky.

Acts 10:10-16 NASB

But he became hungry and was desiring to eat; but while they were making preparations, he fell into a trance; and he *saw the sky opened up, and an object like a great sheet coming down, lowered by four corners to the ground, and there were in it all kinds of four-footed animals and crawling creatures of the earth and birds of the air. A voice came to him, "Get up, Peter, kill and eat!" But Peter said, "By no means, Lord, for I have never eaten anything unholy and unclean." Again a voice came to him a second time, "What God has cleansed, no longer consider unholy." This happened three times, and immediately the object was taken up into the sky.

Revelation 1:10-11 NASB

I was in the Spirit on the Lord's day, and I heard behind me a loud voice like the sound of a trumpet, saying, "Write in a book what you see, and send it to the seven churches: to Ephesus and to Smyrna and to Pergamum and to Thyatira and to Sardis and to Philadelphia and to Laodicea."

You Can Hear God

John 10:27 NASB

My sheep listen to My voice, and I know them, and they follow Me

Philippians 3:15 NASB

Let us therefore, as many as are perfect, have this attitude; and if in anything you have a different attitude, God will reveal that also to you;

Romans 1:20 NASB

For since the creation of the world His invisible attributes, His eternal power and divine nature, have been clearly seen, being understood through what has been made, so that they are without excuse.

Different Ways God Speaks

- **Scripture**
  Psalm 119:105, 2 Timothy 3:16
- **Inner witness**
  Romans 8:16
- **Prophetic words/visions**
  1 Kings 17:8-16, Joel 2:28

- **Circumstances and divine interruptions**
  Acts 16:6–8

- **Dreams and symbols**
  Genesis 40-41, Job 33:14–18, Daniel 2, Acts 16:9–10

- **Creation and conscience**
  Psalms 19:1-4, Romans 1:19-20

- **Angelic messengers**
  Luke 1:11-19, Acts 27:23-24

- **Audible voice**
  1 Samuel 3:4-14, Acts 9:4

The Nature of God's Voice

- **Gentle, not forceful**
  1 Kings 19:12-13 – the still small voice

- **Peaceful, not chaotic**
  Colossians 3:15, Galatians 5:22-23

- **Consistent with His Word**
  2 Timothy 3:16, Romans 3:4

- **Draws you closer, not away**
  John 6:68, Luke 19:48

- **Convicts (not condemns)**
  Luke 19:1-9, Judges 6:11-12)

Common Ways to Hear God

MODE	DESCRIPTION	EXAMPLES
Inner Knowing	Thoughts, pictures, or impressions that comes with insight and peace	"Suddenly I felt so much peace and I just knew God would make a way for us"
Scriptural Highlighting	Bible verse seems like it leaps off the page	"This passage is for me right now."
Dreams/ Visions	Visual messages, often symbolic	"I've had three dreams this week about buying a house."
Prophetic Words	Spoken through others, but produce a sense of confirmation in your spirit	"My heart leaped when he spoke about what God is calling me into."
Audible Voice	Rare, but clear and unmistakable	"Then out loud I heard God say, "Do not take that job."
Creation/ Nature	God revealing His nature through what He's made	"When I saw the sunrise on the ocean, I just started weeping at the beauty of God's creation."

Tuning Your Spiritual Ears

- **Quiet the noise**
  (fasting, rest, solitude)

- **Read and study the Bible**
  Colossians 3:15, Galatians 5:22-23

- **Worship and create space to commune with God**
  2 Timothy 3:16, Romans 3:4

- **Pray and dialogue with God; Ask Him questions**
  John 6:68, Luke 19:48

- **Journal impressions, pictures, and recurring thoughts**
  Luke 19:1-9, Judges 6:11-12)

- **Test what you hear:** *Does it align with Scripture, bear witness, produce fruit?*

Obstacles to Hearing

- **Unforgiveness or bitterness**
  Mark 11:25

- **Fear and unbelief**
  James 1:6

- **Busyness and distraction**
  Luke 10:38-42

- **Relying only on external validation**
  1 Kings 13:7-22

- **Not stewarding what you have already heard**
  Matthew 13:12

Testing What You Hear

- Does it line up with scripture?

- Does it glorify Jesus?

- Does it bear fruit in your life?

- Do wise, mature believers confirm it?

- Does it bring peace and not confusion?

Testing What You Hear

- Be obedient, obedience unlocks greater revelation

- Write it down and review it often
- Pray into it and ask God for more direction or understanding
- Share it with trusted others when you feel led to do so
- Watch for signs of confirmation and await God's timing

A Prayer for Hearing God's Voice

"Lord, I believe You speak to Your children. Open my ears to hear You clearly. Remove distractions, increase my discernment, and teach me to recognize Your voice. I surrender my thoughts, fears, and expectations. Speak, Lord, for Your servant is listening. Amen."

SUPERNATURAL ENCOUNTERS

UNDERSTANDING THE WAYS GOD REVEALS HIMSELF

Throughout Scripture, God reveals Himself to people in profound and personal ways—through dreams, visions, audible voices, angelic visitations, and supernatural experiences. This guide will help you identify, categorize, and steward these encounters with wisdom and reverence.

For free guides and resources, scan this qr code to download the Sons of Prophets app.

BIBLICAL FOUNDATION

Supernatural Encounters

Genesis 28:12 NASB

And he had a dream, and behold, a ladder was set up on the earth with its top reaching to heaven; and behold, the angels of God were ascending and descending on it.

Acts 12:7 NASB

And behold, an angel of the Lord suddenly stood near Peter, and a light shone in the cell; and he struck Peter's side and woke him, saying, "Get up quickly." And his chains fell off his hands.

Luke 1:11–13 NASB

And an angel of the Lord appeared to him, standing to the right of the altar of incense. Zacharias was troubled when he saw the angel, and fear gripped him. But the angel said to him, "Do not be afraid, Zacharias, for your petition has been heard, and your wife Elizabeth will bear you a son, and you will give him the name John.

2 Corinthians 12:2–4 NASB

I know a man in Christ, who fourteen years ago - whether in the body I do not know, or out of the body I do not know, God knows - such a man was caught up to the third heaven. And I know how such a man - whether in the body or apart from the body I do not know, God knows - was caught up into Paradise and heard inexpressible words, which a man is not permitted to speak.

Revelation 1:10-11 NASB

I was in the Spirit on the Lord's day, and I heard behind me a loud voice like the sound of a trumpet, saying, "Write in a book what you see, and send it to the seven churches: to Ephesus and to Smyrna and to Pergamum and to Thyatira and to Sardis and to Philadelphia and to Laodicea."

1 Kings 19:11–12 NASB

So He said, "Go forth and stand on the mountain before the Lord." And behold, the Lord was passing by! And a great and strong wind was rending the mountains and breaking in pieces the rocks before the Lord; but the Lord was not in the wind. And after the wind an earthquake, but the Lord was not in the earthquake. After the earthquake a fire, but the Lord was not in the fire; and after the fire a sound of a gentle blowing.

Types of Encounter

- **Visions**
  Spiritual sight while awake, ranging from subtle impressions to open, cinematic experiences.
  Ezekiel 1, Acts 10, Acts 16:9

- **Dreams**
  Night-time visions or symbolic messages while sleeping
  Genisis 37, Matthew 1-2

- **Visitations**
  Direct manifestation of God, angels, or heavenly beings
  Luke 1, Acts 9, Matthew 17

- **Translations and Transportations**
  Supernatural movement from one location to another, either in the spirit or physically
  Acts 8:39–40, Revelation 4:1–2

- **Audible Voice**
  Heard with natural ears, or so inwardly clear that it seems audible
  1 Samuel 3, Matthew 3:17

Types of Visions

- **Internal/Inner Vision**
  Mental pictures or flashes seen in your mind

- **External/Open Vision**
  Like watching a movie - seen with physical eyes in the natural realm

- **Trance**
  A vision during a state of suspended natural awareness

- **Panoramic Vision**
  A longer, unfolding scene or narrative

- **Night Vision**
  Visions that come in the night while semi-conscious or between waking and sleep

Types of Dreams

- **Symbolic** (metaphoric or poetic)

- **Literal** (direct message)

- **Warning** (from God)

- **Prophetic Destiny** (from God)

- **Soul Dreams** (from self/the flesh)

- **Demonic Nightmares** (from the enemy)

Types of Visitations

- **Jesus**
  Acts 9

- **Holy Spirit**
  Matthew 3:16

- **Angelic**
  Luke 1

- **Other Heavenly Beings or Saints**
  Matthew 17

- **Demonic**
  Matthew 4:1–11

- **Witch/Warlock/Sorcerer**
  Ezekiel 13:17–18, 20–21

How to respond to visitations?

Visitations can produce holy fear, ungodly fear, awe & wonder, quickening or urgency. Rather than only sensing the presence of another, you become vary aware as the evidence is visible and tangible. No matter that visitor, always respond by communicating with God, obeying His voice, and taking authority when needed.

Translation and Transportation

"He stretched out the form of a hand and caught me by a lock of my head; and the Spirit lifted me up between earth and heaven and brought me in the visions of God to Jerusalem, to the entrance of the north gate of the inner court, where the seat of the idol of jealousy, which provokes to jealousy, was located. - Ezekiel 8:3"

- **Physical Relocation by the Spirit**
  Instant physical relocation from one place to another without natural travel.
  Acts 8:39

- **Spiritual or Visionary Travel**
  The Holy Spirit carries a person's spirit or consciousness to another realm or location in vision, revelation, or encounter (the body remains in the same location).
  Revelation 4:2, 21:10

- **Translation by Faith**
  broader term describing a person being moved, transformed, or preserved through faith - divine transition beyond human limitation.
  Hebrews 11:5

Discerning between Encounter, Imagination, and Deception

Remain both honest and childlike, not doubting, but neither assuming. The Holy Spirit helps us to discern between genuine encounters, imaginations, and deception.

Encounter	Experiencing another spiritual being - whether God (producing truth, peace, revelation, godly fear, warning, urgency, alignment with Scripture) or dark powers (producing ungodly fear, confusion, distortion, or bondage, wickedness).
Imagination	Can be vain, or can be sanctified, inspired, or creative - but must be tested and discerned before being treated as revelation.
Deception	A false or manipulative experience (spiritual or mental) that distorts truth and leads away from God's character, Word, or fruit of the Spirit.

Stewarding Encounters

- **Journal**
  Write what you see and hear so revelation isn't forgotten or distorted.

- **Seek Interpretation**
  Share your experiences with trusted leaders for wisdom and accountability.

- **Wait for Timing and Further Clarity**
  Don't rush to act on revelation; let God unfold meaning and season

- **Guard Against Pride or Sensationalism**
  Stay humble, remembering that experiences serve God's purpose, not self-promotion.

A Prayer to Ask for Encounters

"Lord, draw me into deeper encounters with you and allow me to experience a raw and reverent supernatural life. Let every encounter come by Your Spirit, and guard my heart from deception."

Understanding the Prophetic

Cultivating a Lifestyle of Divine Communication

The prophetic is not reserved for a select few. This guide will help demystify the prophetic, grounding it in Scripture, and empowering believers to embrace the voice of the Holy Spirit.

For free guides and resources, scan this qr code to download the **Sons of Prophets app**.

Biblical Foundation

God's Desire to Speak

Numbers 12:6 NASB

He said, "Hear now My words: If there is a prophet among you, I, the Lord, shall make Myself known to him in a vision. I shall speak with him in a dream.

John 16:13 NASB

But when He, the Spirit of truth, comes, He will guide you into all the truth; for He will not speak on His own initiative, but whatever He hears, He will speak; and He will disclose to you what is to come.

Amos 3:7 NASB

Surely the Lord God does nothing unless He reveals His secret counsel to His servants the prophets.

The Source of Prophecy

2 Peter 1:21 NASB

for no prophecy was ever made by an act of human will, but men moved by the Holy Spirit spoke from God.

Revelation 19:10 NASB

Then I fell at his feet to worship him. But he *said to me, "Do not do that; I am a fellow servant of yours and your brethren who hold the testimony of Jesus; worship God. For the testimony of Jesus is the spirit of prophecy."

The Purpose of Prophecy

Direction (guide movements & decisions)

Acts 13:2-3 NASB

While they were ministering to the Lord and fasting, the Holy Spirit said, "Set apart for Me Barnabas and Saul for the work to which I have called them." Then, when they had fasted and prayed and laid their hands on them, they sent them away.

Correction (inspire repentance & realignment)

Jeremiah 25:4-5 NASB

And the Lord has sent to you all His servants the prophets again and again, but you have not listened nor inclined your ear to hear, saying, 'Turn now everyone from his evil way and from the evil of your deeds, and dwell on the land which the Lord has given to you and your forefathers forever and ever;

Revelation *(reveal God's plans & intentions)*

1 Corinthians 14:24–25 NASB

But if all prophesy, and an unbeliever or an ungifted man enters, he is convicted by all, he is called to account by all; the secrets of his heart are disclosed; and so he will fall on his face and worship God, declaring that God is certainly among you.

Encouragement *(strengthen the body of Christ)*

1 Corinthians 14:3 NASB

But one who prophesies speaks to men for edification and exhortation and consolation.

Prophetic Operation

- **Spoken words** & declaration
- **Symbolic** & metaphorical "prophetic acts"
- **Written** prophecies, poems, & parables
- **Creative** expressions
- **Impartation** through supernatural encounters

Prophetic Abilities & Roles

Distinctions can be made in the definition & operation of the spirit of prophecy, the gift of prophecy, the function of a prophet, & the office of a prophet

Spirit of prophecy	Operating under the Spirit's influence/a prophetic atmosphere, even without possessing a gift or office (1 Samuel 10:10)
Gift of prophecy	Operating from your own gift - available to all believers through the work of the Holy Spirit (1 Corinthians 14:31)
Prophet (function)	Operating maturely in prophetic revelation, direction, and discernment - carrying a grace that ushers in the spirit of prophecy, often in intercession for the church (Acts 11:28, Acts 21:10–11)
Prophet (office)	A functioning prophet with official leadership role within the church (Ephesians 4:11). Authority, governance, and responsibility (Acts 13:1, Acts 15:32)

New Testament Prophetic Culture

- **Jesus as the Model**
  John 5:19

- **Prophecy Centered around Christ**
  Revelation 19:10

- **Communal Discernment**
  1 Thessalonians 5:20-21

- **Prophetic Accountability**
  Galatians 2:2

- **Proper Motives**
  1 Corinthians 13:2, 2 Peter 2:1–3

- **Edification of Others**
  1 Corinthians 14:12, Ephesians 4:29

How to Grow in the Prophetic

- Cultivate intimacy with God
- Practice listening and obeying
- Learn prophetic language and symbols
- Serve in your local community
- Study the word of God

Common Misconceptions

MYTH	TRUTH
Prophecy is always about the future	Many prophecies reveal the present or expose the heart
God's voice will be loud and your response must be dramatic to be prophetic	God often speaks gently and through subtle impressions
Mistakes disqualify you	Growth and maturity come through humility and learning

Prophetic Company

God is raising up a people who hear His voice and carry His heart. Prophecy isn't about performance - it's about relationship, obedience, and love. True prophecy is about partnering with the right source, the Spirit of God. It's important to remember that you don't have to be a prophet to be prophetic.

INCREASING SPIRITUAL AWARENESS

A PRACTICAL GUIDE TO SHARPENING YOUR SPIRITUAL SENSES

Perceive, discern, and respond to the movements of God and the spiritual realm. Grow in sensitivity and partnership with the Holy Spirit.

For free guides and resources, scan this qr code to download the Sons of Prophets app.

Biblical Foundation

What Is Spiritual Awareness?

The capacity to sense and understand spiritual realities, atmospheres, and divine promptings.

Hebrews 5:13-14 NASB

For everyone who partakes only of milk is not accustomed to the word of righteousness, for he is an infant. But solid food is for the mature, who because of practice have their senses trained to discern good and evil.

Spiritual Senses

- **Sight**
  Seeing visions, images, or spiritual realities
  Jeremiah 1:11–12, 2 Kings 6:17

- **Hearing**
  Hearing God's voice or angelic messages
  John 10:27

- **Smell**
  Discernment through fragrances (good or evil)
  2 Corinthians 2:15–16

- **Taste**
  Physically tasting or experiencing spiritual realities
  Psalm 34:8

- **Touch**
  Feeling spiritual entities, whether demonic or angelic presence
  Mark 5:30

- **Knowing**
  Inner knowledge or sense of spiritual activity in environment
  Nehemiah 6:12

Barriers to Spiritual Awareness

- **Unbelief or doubt**
  2 Corinthians 4:4

- **Busyness and distraction**
  Luke 10:41, Revelation 2:4

- **Sin or spiritual dullness**
  Hebrews 5:11

- **Over-reliance on logic or intellect**
  1 Corinthians 1:27

- **Fear of deception**
  1 Corinthians 12:1-3

Increasing Spiritual Awareness

- **Cultivate Intimacy with God**
  - Daily worship and prayer
  - Stillness and waiting in God's presence

- **Study the Word with Expectation**
  - Scripture opens your eyes to patterns of how God moves
  - Ask the Holy Spirit to illuminate truth

- **Practice Discernment**
  - Test atmospheres, voices, and motives
  - Ask God questions in real-time
  - Journal impressions and confirmations

- **Train Your Spiritual Senses**
  - Engage in quiet reflection and listening
  - Try "spiritual observation" exercises
  - Ask God what He's doing in moments

- **Fast and Consecrate Your Focus**
  - Fasting sharpens awareness by reducing fleshly distractions
  - Consecration and obedience creates a sensitivity to the Holy Spirit's leadings

Discerning Atmospheres

- The Presence of Peace vs. Oppression
- Angelic Activity vs. Demonic Interference
- Moments of Divine Invitation or Warning

Grow in Community

- Share what you perceive with trusted mentors
- Receive correction and sharpening from others
- Avoid isolation and spiritual elitism

Steward Spiritual Intel

- Record your dreams and visions
- Journal sudden thoughts, impressions, or unusual emotions
- Learn to distinguish God's voice from your own thoughts or whispers from the enemy

Final Encouragement

Spiritual awareness grows best in humility, wonder, and dependence on God - not striving or fear of missing out.

"Blessed are the pure in heart, for they shall see God...." - Matthew 5:8

DREAM
INTERPRETATION

INTRODUCTORY GUIDE TO INTERPRET REVELATORY DREAMS

God often speaks through dreams, revealing messages, warnings, and guidance. This guide helps you discern, interpret, and steward those divine revelations.

For free guides and resources, scan this qr code to download the **Sons of Prophets app.**

BIBLICAL FOUNDATION

God Speaks Through Dreams

Numbers 12:6 NASB

He said, "Hear now My words: If there is a prophet among you, I, the Lord, shall make Myself known to him in a vision. I shall speak with him in a dream.

Dreams Require Interpretation

Genesis 40:8 NASB

Then they said to him, "We have had a dream and there is no one to interpret it." Then Joseph said to them, "Do not interpretations belong to God? Tell it to me, please."

Daniel 1:17 NASB

As for these four youths, God gave them knowledge and intelligence in every branch of literature and wisdom; Daniel even understood all kinds of visions and dreams.

The Purpose of Dreams

Divine Communication (*guide movements & decisions*)

Job 33:14–16 NASB

"Indeed God speaks once,
Or twice, yet no one notices it.
"In a dream, a vision of the night,
When sound sleep falls on men,
While they slumber in their beds,
Then He opens the ears of men,
And seals their instruction,

Spiritual Insight

Matthew 2:12 NASB

And having been warned by God in a dream not to return to Herod, the magi left for their own country by another way.

1 Corinthians 2:10–11 NASB

For to us God revealed them through the Spirit; for the Spirit searches all things, even the depths of God. For who among men knows the thoughts of a man except the spirit of the man which is in him? Even so the thoughts of God no one knows except the Spirit of God.

Types of Dreams

• Prophetic

Warning: *Potential danger for you, family, nations, or the world*
(Matthew 2:12)

Guidance: *Instructions that often demand sudden obedience*
(Acts 16:9)

Strategy: *Ideas, answers or new wisdom to approach situations*
(Psalm 127:1)

Impartation: *Receiving blessing, gifts, inheritance, and transfers at night*
(1 Kings 3:5)

• Processing

Gates: *Your mind is reviewing heavy impressions through eye and ear gates that haven't been flushed before sleeping*
(Psalm 101:3)

Training: *Chewing the cud, evaluating bits of revelation from the Lord to grow in knowledge*
(Galatians 5:16)

- ## Warfare
  __Attack__: Enemy accusation, torment, depression, and tear-down. Nightmares and sleep terrors
  (Psalm 91)
  __Discernment__: Seeing the truth about something you'll have to confront. Fight that challenges your mission
  (Ephesians 5:6-10)

- ## Soulish
  __Fears__: Hurt, doubt, or lack of trust could be ruling you. Need more Bible foundations
  (Isaiah 41:10)
  __Passions__: Hidden desire, sin, or not enough time walking in the Spirit
  (Galatians 5:16)
  __Guilt__: Need to confess something to God and trustworthy counselors/fellow believers
  (James 5:16, 1 John 1:9)

How to Interpret a Dream

1. **Write it Down**
   Record it immediately upon waking

2. **Pray First**
   Ask the Holy Spirit to bring clarity

3. **Identify Symbols**
   Look at key people, objects, locations, and emotions

4. **Use Scripture**
   Look for parallels in the Bible

5. **Discern the Source**
   Is it from God, the soul, or the enemy?

6. **Remove Yourself**
   Consider if the dream is about someone else - is God revealing a point of intercession?

7. **Seek Counsel**
   Allow trusted voices in community to weigh in when you feel it's necessary

8. **Wait and Hold**
   Not all dreams may be immediately clear, some may be understood in time and as you seek the Lord.

Dream Symbols

These are not meant to be your direct guide to interpret dream symbols, as the meaning often changes. But to give an example, here are a few commonly interpreted symbols:

MYTH	TRUTH
Water	Holy Spirit, cleansing, the Word of God
Snakes	Deception, demonic influence
Vehicles	Ministry, life journey, calling
Babies	New beginnings, assignments, or immaturity
Loosing teeth	Insecurity, loss of wisdom or confidence

Emotions in Dreams

The emotions you feel during a dream are often a key to interpretation. Ask:

- Did I feel peace or fear?
- Was the tone corrective, instructive, or comforting?
- Was I an observer or a participant?

Recurring Dreams

Recurring dreams often highlight:

- An unresolved issue
- A spiritual calling or assignment
- A divine warning that hasn't been heeded

Testing What You Hear

- Does it line up with scripture?
- Does it glorify Jesus?
- Does it bear fruit in your life?
- Do wise, mature believers confirm it?
- Does it bring peace and not confusion?

Tools for Dream Interpretation

- Dream Journals
- Scrap Paper (for processing before journaling)
- Study Bible

Final Thoughts

Dreams are not just mystical experiences, they are invitations to conversation with God. Interpretation is not just about decoding symbols, but discerning the heart of the Father. Your dreams matter, and the precess of stewarding them can be enriching, rewarding, and help you grow in spiritual discernment.

HOW TO BREAK WITCHCRAFT

STAND IN AUTHORITY AGAINST SPIRITUAL MANIPULATION

Whether through cauldrons and curses, or any attempt to control, manipulate, or influence others through soulish or dark spiritual practices, learn to stand against rebellion and spiritual domination.

For free guides and resources, scan this qr code to download the **Sons of Prophets app**.

BIBLICAL FOUNDATION

Witchcraft is Rebellion

1 Samuel 15:23 NASB

"For rebellion is as the sin of divination,
And insubordination is as iniquity and idolatry.
Because you have rejected the word of the Lord,
He has also rejected you from being king."

Witchcraft is Detestable

Deuteronomy 18:10–14 NASB

There shall not be found among you anyone who
makes his son or his daughter pass through the fire,
one who uses divination, one who practices witchcraft,
or one who interprets omens, or a sorcerer, or one
who casts a spell, or a medium, or a spiritist, or one
who calls up the dead. For whoever does these things
is detestable to the Lord; and because of these
detestable things the Lord your God will drive them
out before you. You shall be blameless before the Lord
your God. For those nations, which you shall
dispossess, listen to those who practice witchcraft and
to diviners, but as for you, the Lord your God has not
allowed you to do so.

Witchcraft is a Work of the Flesh

Galatians 5:19–21 NASB

Now the deeds of the flesh are evident, which are: immorality, impurity, sensuality, idolatry, sorcery, enmities, strife, jealousy, outbursts of anger, disputes, dissensions, factions, envying, drunkenness, carousing, and things like these, of which I forewarn you, just as I have forewarned you, that those who practice such things will not inherit the kingdom of God.

2 Corinthians 10:4–5NASB

for the weapons of our warfare are not of the flesh, but divinely powerful for the destruction of fortresses. We are destroying speculations and every lofty thing raised up against the knowledge of God, and we are taking every thought captive to the obedience of Christ,

Acts 19:18–20 NASB

Many also of those who had believed kept coming, confessing and disclosing their practices. And many of those who practiced magic brought their books together and began burning them in the sight of everyone; and they counted up the price of them and found it fifty thousand pieces of silver. So the word of the Lord was growing mightily and prevailing.

Forms of Witchcraft

- **Occult Witchcraft**
  Traditional practices (spells, curses, rituals, necromancy)

- **Religious Witchcraft**
  Control masked in spiritual language, legalism, false prophecy

- **Soulish Witchcraft**
  Manipulation or coercion by emotional pressure or willpower

- **Charasmatic Witchcraft**
  Misuse of gifts to control people or outcomes ("thus saith the Lord" manipulation)

Common Signs of Witchcraft

- **Sudden** confusion, fogginess, or forgetfulness

- **Unexplainable** fatigue or heaviness

- **Intense** spiritual pressure or torment

- **Relationship** divisions, control, intimidation, & miscommunication

- **Mental** oppression, dreams of snakes, spiders, or shadowy figures
- **Disruption** in prayer, worship, or clarity

Legal Doors That Give Access

- Involvement in occult practices (even past)
- Bitterness, unforgiveness, or rebellion
- Exposure to spiritually toxic materials (books, shows, objects)
- Word curses and agreements with lies

Breaking Witchcraft

1. Submit to God

- Submit to God. Resist the devil and he will flee (*James 4:7*)
- Repent of any open doors or spiritual compromise

2. Break Agreements and Curses

- Verbally renounce any word curses, control, or manipulation

- Break soul ties and ungodly alignments
- Cancel all spoken or unspoken agreements in Jesus' name *(Philippians 2:10-11)*

3. Declare the Word of God

- Isaiah 54:17 – "No weapon formed against you shall prosper…"
- Revelation 12:11 – "They overcame by the blood of the Lamb…"
- Philippians 2:10-11 – "That at the name of Jesus every knee should bow…"

4. Command Witchcraft to Break

- With authority, speak directly to the assignment: *"In the name of Jesus, I break every form of witchcraft, manipulation, control, and spiritual confusion. Go now."*

5. Restore Clarity and Presence

- Invite the Holy Spirit to fill the space again
- Worship and pray in tongues to restore spiritual atmosphere
- Anoint your space if necessary

Practical Protection Steps

- Keep your environment spiritually clean
- Be careful of who lays hands on you or speaks into your life
- Disentangle from spiritual manipulators— even subtly religious ones
- Be watchful of "flattery and favor" used to gain access
- Put on the full armor of God (Ephesians 6:10-18)
- Pray in the Holy Spirit
- Get around community, don't stay isolated

Spiritual Warfare vs. Paranoia

- Walk in discernment, not fear (2 Timothy 1:7)
- Not everything is witchcraft—check your soul before labeling others
- Be careful not to accuse based on emotion or suspicion

Dealing with People Operating in Witchcraft

- Confront, if led, with love and truth (Matthew 18)
- Do not retaliate - bless and set boundaries
- Cut soul ties and remove spiritual influence
- Pray for their repentance but guard your atmosphere

Stay Rooted in the Spirit, Not Reaction

Witchcraft loses power when you:
- Stay in worship
- Maintain peace
- Anchor in the Word
- Don't fight in the flesh

"For the weapons of our warfare are not of the flesh, but divinely powerful for the destruction of fortresses."

-2 Corinthians 10:4

DEALING WITH DEMONIC SPIRITS

A GUIDE TO DISCERNMENT, AUTHORITY, AND FREEDOM

Deliverance was central to Jesus' ministry and remains a core part of ours. This guide equips you to discern demonic activity, understand biblical authority, and walk in freedom with wisdom and confidence.

BIBLICAL FOUNDATION

Authority Over Demons

Mark 16:17 NASB

These signs will accompany those who have believed: in My name they will cast out demons, they will speak with new tongues;

Luke 10:19 NASB

Behold, I have given you authority to tread on serpents and scorpions, and over all the power of the enemy, and nothing will injure you.

Matthew 10:1 NASB

Jesus summoned His twelve disciples and gave them authority over unclean spirits, to cast them out, and to heal every kind of disease and every kind of sickness.

Matthew 12:28 NASB

But if I cast out demons by the Spirit of God, then the kingdom of God has come upon you.

Armor & Resistance

James 4:7 NASB

Submit therefore to God. Resist the devil and he will flee from you.

Ephesians 4:27 NASB

and do not give the devil an opportunity.

Ephesians 6:10–17 NASB

Finally, be strong in the Lord and in the strength of His might. Put on the full armor of God, so that you will be able to stand firm against the schemes of the devil. For our struggle is not against flesh and blood, but against the rulers, against the powers, against the world forces of this darkness, against the spiritual forces of wickedness in the heavenly places. Therefore, take up the full armor of God, so that you will be able to resist in the evil day, and having done everything, to stand firm. Stand firm therefore, having girded your loins with truth, and having put on the breastplate of righteousness, and having shod your feet with the preparation of the gospel of peace; in addition to all, taking up the shield of faith with which you will be able to extinguish all the flaming arrows of the evil one. And take the helmet of salvation, and the sword of the Spirit, which is the word of God.

Understanding Deliverance

Definition

The act of casting out or breaking free from demonic influence, oppression, or possession in the soul (mind, will, emotions) or the body.

Jesus' Example

"When evening came, they brought to Him many who were demon-possessed; and He cast out the spirits with a word, and healed all who were ill."

- Matthew 8:16 NASB

Our Commission

"He who has believed and has been baptized shall be saved; but he who has disbelieved shall be condemned. These signs will accompany those who have believed: in My name they will cast out demons, they will speak with new tongues; they will pick up serpents, and if they drink any deadly poison, it will not hurt them; they will lay hands on the sick, and they will recover."

- Mark 16:16-18

Signs of Demonic Influence

- Persistent tormenting thoughts or emotions
- Compulsive behavior or addictions
- Chronic fear, heaviness, or oppression
- Unexplainable sickness or paralysis
- Resistance to prayer, Scripture, or worship
- Voice changes, contortions, or superhuman strength (in more extreme cases)

Levels of Demonic Influence

MYTH	TRUTH
Oppression	External pressure, torment, or harassment
Obsession	Mental and emotional domination or control
Possession	Full or partial inhabitation of the body, soul, or bloodline
Strongholds	Belief systems or patterns of thought that give demons a legal right to influence

Common Spirits and their Traits

- **Spirit of Fear**
  Torment, anxiety, paranoia (2 Timothy 1:7)

- **Spirit of Rejection**
  Self-hate, isolation, bitterness

- **Spirit of Lust**
  Unclean thoughts, sexual addiction, perversion

- **Spirit of Witchcraft**
  Control, rebellion, confusion

- **Spirit of Heaviness**
  Depression, suicide, fatigue

- **Religious Spirit**
  Legalism, judgment, pride

- **Spirit of Infirmity**
  Sickness, pain, pity seeking

- **Pagan / Ritual Spirits**
  Ishtar, Lucifer

What Deliverance is Not:

- A one-time cure for everything
- An emotional spectacle
- A replacement for discipleship or counseling
- Something to fear or idolize

Ministering in Deliverance

1. Preparation

- The deliverance minister should should walk in purity and authority, be submitted to God, and fast and pray beforehand as led by the Holy Spirit (Mark 9:29).

- The person receiving ministry should walk through confession, repentance, and forgiveness (Mark 11:25)

2. Discernment

Ask the Holy Spirit what spirit(s) may be present. Pay attention to your spiritual senses and listen to God-given instinct.

3. Legal Grounds

Identify open doors: sin, trauma, unforgiveness, occult activity either prophetically, by asking the person direct questions to receive direct answers

4. Renunciation

Lead the person through verbally rejecting and canceling agreement with those spirits

5. Command

With authority, command the spirit(s) to leave in Jesus' name. It's not about your authority alone, but the authority of Christ.

6. Expulsion

The spirit may leave with manifestations (coughing, shaking, crying, etc.). Do not be overwhelmed or impressed by ongoing, unnecessary manifestations. Take authority and command the demon(s) to leave.

7. Filling

Pray for the Holy Spirit to fill the person and seal every area with the blood of Jesus.

8. Discipleship

Teach the person how to maintain freedom, to be transformed by the renewing of their mind (Romans 12:2), and to resist any demonic spirit that might try to return later (James 4:7).

Remaining Free After Deliverance

- Daily intimacy with God
- Renewing the mind with truth of the Bible
- Close community and accountability
- Guarding your heart and lifestyle
- Protecting your senses, guarding your eyes and ears (gates. Matthew 6:22)
- Breaking all soul ties, occult objects, and former agreements

Cautions and Wisdom

- Don't confront principalities unless led by the Holy Spirit
- Don't willfully engage in deliverance if you're spiritually compromised
- Don't glorify the demonic - glorify Jesus
- Know your authority and boundaries, bring others into the picture as needed.

Can a Christian Have a Demon?

This is one of the most frequently asked - and most misunderstood - questions in deliverance ministry. The Short answer is: **Yes, a Christian can have a demon - but perhaps not in the way people often assume.**

The Myth: "A Demon Can't Live Where the Holy Spirit Dwells"

This idea comes from a misunderstanding of how spiritual influence and human design work. The logic goes: "God is holy. Demons are unclean. Therefore, they cannot coexist." But this isn't biblically or experientially sound.

Let's break it down:

1. Spirit, Soul, and Body

- A believer is a three-part being: spirit, soul, and body (1 Thessalonians 5:23).

- When you're saved, the Holy Spirit takes up residence in your spirit.

- Demonic influence or inhabitation does not happen in your spirit - it can exist in the soul (mind, emotions) or body.

- Think of it this way: a demon can live in the house, but it can't sit on the throne unless you let it.

2. Biblical Evidence of Christians Needing Deliverance

- Paul writes to believers: "Do not give the devil a foothold" (Ephesians 4:27). He's not warning unbelievers - he's warning Christians.

- The Corinthian church was filled with spiritual gifts (1 Corinthians 1:7) yet was heavily influenced by sexual immorality, idolatry, and division. Paul rebukes them and calls them to purity (1 Corinthians 5).

- Believers are told to "cast down imaginations" and "take every thought captive" (2 Corinthians 10:5) - because spiritual strongholds can exist even in a redeemed mind.

2. Real-World Analogy

Saying "a Christian can't have a demon because they have the Holy Spirit" is like saying:

- "A Christian can't get sick because Jesus is the Healer."
- "A Christian can't sin because they're a new creation."

Yet most Christians can admit they've gotten sick and have wrestled with sin, many still needing freedom. Deliverance isn't about salvation - it's about sanctification and alignment.

3. The Enemy Seeks Territory

- Even if a demon can't own you through possession, it still wants access, and even to take territory by taking up residence.
- Christians can open doors through sin, trauma, or occult exposure, leave strongholds unchecked, allowing demonic footholds, and ignore spiritual warfare, giving the enemy legal rights to operate.

Final Thoughts

True deliverance brings people into the freedom Jesus paid for. It's not about the theatrics - it's about compassion, wholeness, and the advancing the Kingdom of God.

You can be saved and Spirit-filled and still need deliverance. It's not a contradiction - it's part of the journey of total freedom.

Needing deliverance is not a sign of spiritual failure. It's a sign that God loves us too much to leave us in bondage.

"So if the Son makes you free, you will be free indeed." - *John 8:36*

CREATED BY

RICKY BROWN   LISA KOCHER

SONS OF PROPHETS

www.ingramcontent.com/pod-product-compliance
Lightning Source LLC
Chambersburg PA
CBHW041630140626
46547CB00032B/2514